The U.S. Struggle

for

Global Hegemony

The Business Model

Basic strategic features and the strategic global spheres

by

Georg von Goldbach

AF191520

This book is a revised version of
Part Three - Chapter 2 of the book

Europe on the Way to her Apocalypse
History – Background – Perspectives

Bibliographic information from the German
National Library:
The German National Library lists this
publication in the German National Bibliography;
detailed bibliographic data are available online at
https://dnb.de.
ISBN
Copyright (2024) Engelsdorfer Verlag Leipzig
All rights reserved by the author
Manufactured in Leipzig, Germany (EU)
www.engelsdorfer-verlag.de
Euro (Germany)

© 2024 Georg von Goldbach
Verlag: BoD • Books on Demand GmbH, In de
Tarpen 42, 22848 Norderstedt
Druck: Libri Plureos GmbH, Friedensallee 273,
22763 Hamburg
ISBN: 978-3-7597-5080-8

Inhalt

The Book put into context

This book can confirm what many have known for a long time, namely that historiography... is the record of the crimes and madness of humanity. It is no help for prophecies.

The Age of Extremes, World History of the 20th Century
Eric Hobsbawm

What's at stake: the Apocalypse

"If – God forbid – such a war takes place, it will not follow the scenario of a special military operation. It will not be conducted in trenches with artillery, armored vehicles, drones and radio-electronic defense."

*For the NATO-Russia war to be fought in a conventional way, the balance of power between NATO and Russia is too unequal – NATO is a huge military bloc with a military budget of up to one and a half trillion dollars, i.e. US$1,500,000,000,000,-- and a population of almost one billion people. Because of this incomparability, Russia has no choice but to give an **"asymmetrical response"**:*

"Ballistic missiles and cruise missiles with special warheads are being used to defend the territorial integrity of our country."

Security Council of the Russian Federation, 06.02.2024
Warning of a Nuclear War, Dmitry Medvedev

FOREWORD

The personal motivation for this book comes from my realization that the creation of peace is, in our time, the most important concern of humanity. I was born in Germany and can therefore say that war is in my blood, as it is the case for most Europeans. A great number of wars have been waged on European ground among the European nations over the past 600 years. In response to that, the European Union has been created and has progressively been shaped after the End of the Second World War as a "peace project". This hope is waning more and more, and Europe does not seem capable of escaping the claws of the evil of war.

In the decades after 1993, I had increasingly worked as a consultant for the European Union (EU). In the beginning, I was very happy and even enthusiastic to do this, as long as the EU's credible intention for "international partnership" was still the guiding principle for the work of our advisory services activities abroad. After 2001, however, I had noticed how an intentional effort for dominance had increasingly come to the fore within the foreign policy of the EU.

Relations with partner countries became increasingly political, less characterized by friendship and the honest dealings among partners. Of course, this change in attitude had also become obvious to many of our partners in the countries in which we worked. I am more of a free and liberal spirit by nature, and ideological narrow-mindedness has never been one of my personal traits. However, I have always endeavored to consciously guide my actions based on my ethical convictions and moral principles.

I can say that peaceful development among people and nations based on shared values and principles has always been a matter close to my heart. That is why I didn't feel challenged in particular when I was asked to consciously and with conviction, but without personal zeal or even fanaticism, to work for the healthy development of Europe and its relations with other countries in the world. My anxiety therefore increased more and more as certain authoritarian tendencies in the EU and the European Commission became more frequently apparent to me. I then drafted an essay in 2017, essentially for myself, to clearly articulate my own thoughts, entitled "How Europe Lost Her Sovereignty". In it, I showed how, in the interplay between Germany and France, which had become a second spiritual home for me, the European Commission usurped the sovereignty of the nation states and increasingly restricted their national responsibility. In addition, as a "participating observer", I had recognized that a war was being prepared on European soil. Of course, that was not easy to see at the time. All the friends, acquaintances and business partners I wanted to point out only looked into the air when I talked about it. Nobody wanted to know anything about it. I myself did not investigate this question and, of course, could not know in what form this war would then begin and take place. I was also personally surprised by the way, with a flick of the wrist, Germany and Europe were driven into this war, which was foreseeable by 2014 at the latest and then turned into an open war in 2022.

Personally, this experience has shaken me very much, also in my trust in people as a whole. I didn't want to believe how sensible and intelligent people could get involved in such stupidity. The experience of this irrationality still pains me very much. My grandfather was sent into the First World War in 1914 with the motto "Cannon thunder is our greeting". My father went to war in 1939 for the Hitler regime, from which he was not to return home from Russian captivity until the end of 1947[1], severely damaged in physical health and also mentally. And now, at the end of my life, the war was to haunt me and perhaps plague my children as well.

I have always consciously enjoyed and never despised the great fortune of growing up in peace and being able to shape my life peacefully. Peace had always seemed to me to be a great and precious good that had to be carefully preserved. Unfortunately, we did not succeed in this.

---

[1] At a time when Russia is once again under strong ideological attack, it is necessary to confess that I have not developed any negative attitude or resentment from my father's experience in the mines of Russia. My father had been a prisoner of war (Kgf) and his imprisonment was therefore the result of a war that had arisen and been waged in a criminal way.

THE SPIRITUAL FATHERS OF THIS BOOK

The intellectual authorship of this book is held by two American thinkers and visionaries. The two have never met in person, but what they have in common is that they derive their thinking from cybernetics in order to understand and explain this world[2]. This is obvious with Gregory Bateson[3], because he speaks of it quite openly in his writings. In the case of R. Buckminster Fuller[4]

---

[2] Cybernetics is the science of controlling and regulating machines in analogy to the functioning of living organisms by means of feedback processes that are receiving impulses by the sense organs. In social organizations, feedback works through information, communication and participant observation. The science of cybernetics was born from the cooperation of scientists of the "Vienna Circle". It was formulated by Norbert Wiener after 1945, after his emigration to the USA, when he came to the realization that intelligent behavior can be described as the result of feedback mechanisms.

[3] In the case of Gregory Bateson, we are essentially referring to the collection of essays published as "Ecology of the Mind" in 1985. The English edition "Steps to an Ecology of Mind, Collected Essays" dates from 1972.

[4] At Buckminster Fuller, our main source is his book "Critical Path", which was published in 1981. Probably

, the reference to cybernetics is visible everywhere in his writings and also in his works, but he was more of a pragmatist and generalist nature. "Bucky" Fuller strove to live a life, in which he fought for the practical implementation of his ideas, mainly through the use and application of his design artefacts, while Gregory Bateson limited himself to theoretical and epistemological reflection and teaching.

What they both have in common is that they were very sharp observers of what was going on in the world and always keen to understand how people acted. Both have always put people at the centre of their efforts and have always put people in a larger, comprehensive context and under a system view. In Buckminster Fuller's case, it was "man in the universe." For Gregory Bateson, it was the systemic relation between man and nature. What both have in common is that they saw the fundamental fallacy in human

---

his best-known book is the "Operating Manual for Spaceship Erath", from 1969. It can be downloaded online from the Buckminster Fuller Institute website. the German edition of "Instruction manual for the spaceship Earth and other writings" dates from 2011.

thought and action in the fact that man saw himself disconnected from these necessary systemic relations with nature and the universe. Both explained this as the result of the one-sided emphasis on the development of the natural sciences since the 17th century, which has led to a mechanistic world view. This paradigm of human isolation from nature and the universe, as both saw it, slowly dissolved again since the early 20th century with quantum mechanics and the understanding of the meaning of the "uncertainty principle". A door had opened. It had become possible to reconnect with the nature of man and his importance in the cosmos.[5] This sums up the experience shared by Gregory Bateson and Buckminster Fuller.

In order to understand these two great minds, we would like to emphasize the decisive basic idea that is characteristic of each of them. Buckminster Fuller developed his first and decisive basic idea from the application of "general principles and laws" to the understanding of the functioning of *man in universe*. He convincingly shows that it is not

---

5 Fritjof Capra gives a catchy account of this in his "Tao of Physics", 1977.

the lack of energy that inhibits the development of humanity. Rather, the fundamental mistake lies in the fact that humanity has not found, not understood, the access to the infinite source of energy that is provided to us from the universe through the sun. This lack of access to understanding eternally regenerating energy has so far kept people being caught in a self-made trap. According to Buckminster Fuller, this phenomenon can be traced back to the work of Malthus, who at the beginning of the 19th century established the principle that humans would reproduce with the necessary fatefulness, but at the same time had only limited natural resources. Hence, the fight for limited resources was inevitable. For Darwin, this became the struggle for existence and lead Darwinists to formulate the principle of the "survival of the fittest". If we take these thoughts just a few steps further, we end up directly at the rationale for the demand for "unlimited growth" of the economy, and at the political level, for the hegemonic striving and the seemingly inevitable wars as a means of gaining power, which are at the center of the critical analysis of our book.

Gregory Bateson is an anthropologist by training. But he has also worked successfully in psychology and psychiatry[6]. However, he has the most important significance as a researcher on epistemology and in particular on the importance of cybernetics for the sciences and for the shaping of human living conditions on earth.

He says of himself that "the two most important historical events in my life were the Treaty of Versailles and the discovery of cybernetics".[7] This certainly sounds astonishing, because it is not immediately clear what the relationship between these two "events" looks like. We come closer to understanding what Gregory Bateson means when he says that, in his view, the "important question for history is: has the default[8] or

---

[6] The term "double-bind", i.e. the relationship trap, was coined by him.

[7] In this part, we essentially refer to Gregory Bateson, "Ecology of the Mind, Part VI, Crises in the Ecology of the Mind, from Versailles to Cybernetics", from his lecture of 1966.

[8] The term "specification" here refers to cybernetics, as a system theory, and means "leadership variable" or "decisive reference value" to which the other parameters and elements of a system are oriented.

attitude been changed?". He goes on to explain that "the most important points in history are... the historical moments... in which attitudes are changed", in which previous "values" change. He then shows that the Treaty of Versailles has not successfully changed the behavior of the most important signatories of the treaty[9], i.e. Germany, France, Great Britain and the USA.[10] Therefore, according to his understanding, the inevitable consequence of the Treaty of Versailles was the Second World War, with the same nations as important protagonists. He calls the Treaty of Versailles one of the "greatest relapses in the history of our civilization" and says that "we will have to deal with the aftermath of this betrayal for a

---

[9] We should note here that since the October Revolution of 1917, a government had taken power in Russia with which the United States did not want to come to an understanding.

[10] As we will show later, it was precisely this thought that guided Rudolf Steiner in his assessment of the events surrounding the First World War. He insisted that it was necessary to change the political "rules" in order not to prepare a new catastrophe. As we know, Max von Baden, the last Reich Chancellor of the German Empire, very soon ended Rudolf Steiner's advisory activities.

number of generations to come", before adding that "betrayal in an armistice or in peace negotiations is worse than a stratagem in battle." His conclusion: "It goes on and on. The tragedy of fluctuating, self-propagating mistrust, hatred and destruction through generations".

Gregory Bateson is aware that cybernetics, i.e. "the second historical event" of his time, will not in itself bring the solution to our geopolitical problems. But he sees that it can be a contribution to changing attitudes and behavior. But he also knows that "any understanding can be used destructively". He summarizes his insight as follows: "In cybernetics itself there is integrity[11], which helps us not to be seduced by it into another madness, but we cannot trust that it will keep us from sin"[12] and then he adds in a more hopeful tone: "But this much is certain, that in cybernetics there is also the means to achieve

---

[11] Because cybernetics allows us to see the connections between events.

[12] We would like to note here that Buckminster Fuller also sees integrity as a very important criterion for good and successful action. That's how he called one of his books "Ideas and Integrities" from 1963. He also emphasizes this point in his "Critical Path".

a new and perhaps human worldview, a means to change our philosophy of power and a means to see our own stupidities in a larger perspective".

THE U.S. STRUGGLE FOR GLOBAL HEGEMONY AS A BUSINESS MODEL

Outline of the basic strategic features of the American struggle for global hegemony

"It is not said that the war will end one day. Of course, there may be a small break. War may have to take a breather, yes, it may have an accident, so to speak. He is not safe from that, there is nothing perfect here on earth."

> The field preacher in "Mother Courage",
> by Bert Brecht

"I believe that only a general renunciation of armed force at all (...) makes sense"

Man and the Atom, Outlook on the Future, 1968[13]
Max Born, Nobel Prize in Physics, 1954.

---

[13] The Nobel Prize winner in physics Max Born was a co-signatory of the Göttingen Manifesto of 1957, in which 18 well-known West German nuclear researchers campaigned against the nuclear armament of the Bundeswehr.

INTRODUCTORY NOTE

With this short essay, we want to encourage readers to let go of illusions and say goodbye to current deceptions.

The main illusion and deception we often indulge in on a global scale is to believe that much of what happens on a global political and economic level is due to chance or bad luck. Also, we often think that many of the armed conflicts and events, in which the U.S. is involved or engaged, are to its detriment and harm it. This may be the case in the long term, which we cannot ultimately assess with certainty. In the short and medium term, however, the United States, with all the wars and conflicts it has initiated and waged globally for centuries, has always pursued its economic and geopolitical interests in a very targeted manner and has obviously achieved them to a considerable extent. This can be seen in its globally dominant role over the past century. It's like in a casino, where they use to say that "the bank always wins". In this short book, we want to show why this is so and how the mechanisms that have ensured the dominant role of the USA are functioning effectively.

Since the end of the British Empire, the USA has been the globally dominant power, and it is in the process of further expanding and consolidating this position by force. If we look at the details of the current and past wars and conflicts, we could also say that the United States is doing this "at any cost", often at the cost of destroying human lives by the hundreds of thousands, or even at the price of destroying the natural environment and recklessly consuming global natural resources.[14]

We should always bear this in mind when looking at the political, military and economic events on earth. The US is primarily pursuing its own national selfish interests, even if this obviously causes great harm to other people and plunges entire countries and nations into misfortune, as was the case in Vietnam, as happened in Syria and Iraq, and as has now been staged on a large scale in Ukraine. The necessary connection between the hegemonic striving of the USA and the

---

[14] In a FAZ podcast from 09.04.2024, Jean-Claude Juncker, long-time President of the EU Commission, sums it up as follows: "One hour of war is more expensive than ten years of the EU".

waging of war is very clearly elaborated in the book "A Century of War: Lincoln, Wilson, and Roosevelt", by John V. Denson. In this book, he also shows how American revisionist historiography repeatedly presents the entire American hegemonic striving as the commitment to "humanism, peace and prosperity".[15]

Behind this foil of the strategy of the zero-sum game[16], in which the gain of one causes necessarily the loss of the other, we must therefore look at all these past and especially the current events.[17] If we do not do this, then

---

[15] "A Century of War" was given in 1997 as a lecture on the fifteenth anniversary of the Ludwig von Mises Institute. "Abraham Lincoln and the First Shot" and "Franklin D. Roosevelt and the First Shot" are from "Reassessing the Presidency: The Rise of the Executive State and the Decline of Freedom" (Auburn, Ala.: Mises Institute, 2001). "The Calamity of World War I" and "Another Century of War?" first appeared in the Freeman, and "The Will to Peace" was originally released on LewRockwell.com, and Mises.org.

[16] A recent article in Foreign Affairs, Volume 103 Number 3, expresses this emblematically. There it says: "No Substitute for Victory", in German one would say: only a victory counts.

[17] It is certainly no coincidence that Chinese foreign policy repeatedly emphasizes the principle of "win-

we are indulging in a dangerous illusion and deception. Russia has just had to learn this lesson bitterly. China has woken up and has now understood that the age of illusions is over.

---

win", i.e. the positive-sum game, in which all participants are seen as equal partners, whose interests are taken into account and who have a right to their own benefit.

CLARIFICATION OF CONCEPTS AND THE LOGIC OF THE US APPROACH IN ITS QUEST FOR GLOBAL HEGEMONY

It is important to be aware in detail of how the US global political strategy for world domination looks like, what its stated goals and intentions are, and how the underlying motives behind it become effective.[18]

So if we ask ourselves what the conscious intentions and goals are, it is in line with the openly professed doctrine of the USA to strive for global political and economic power and dominance, i.e. for global hegemony. The USA wants to politically determine what the individual actors on earth, i.e. the countries and nations, do and according to which rules and principles they function. This is what the

---

[18] Rudolf Steiner expressed fundamental thoughts on the history of Europe and on historical symptomatology as a necessary method of historical science in lectures he gave in various European countries and cities in the years after the First World War. For an approach to his understanding of history, volume GA 335 of the Rudolf Steiner Complete Edition is recommended, where he also speaks of an "English-political ideal of world domination born out of the unconscious".

US means by "rules-based world order".[19] The US is concerned with exercising this hegemonic power in order to force other countries and nations to adopt a "rules-based world order" according to the ideas of the USA. It must be noted that the USA itself often does not meet the requirements of this human rights based model of the rule of law.[20]

For the USA, this hegemony also includes unrestricted power over the financial and productive resources in the world. Countries and nations are to pay part of their economic output to the United States in a consistent manner and without objection. This

---

[19] "Rules-based World Order, Around the World in 80 Phrases", 01 July 2020, by Jörg Lau.

[20] On the role of the CIA, you can find articles and lectures by Jeffry Sachs here: https://www.jeffsachs.org/newspaper-articles/yhhc8kcdnmhj4gphzwp387wkgt56c2; elsewhere notes on the war in Ukraine: https://www.jeffsachs.org/newspaper-articles/tag/Ukraine. In Noam Chomsky's case, we find examples of Israel and Palestine in which the zero-sum game of American foreign policy becomes clear: e.g. here: https://www.deutschlandfunk.de/offene-wunde-nahost-israel-die-palaestinenser-und-die-us-100.html

corresponds to a kind of "tribute"[21] that the US claims in reward for its worldwide efforts to promote "peace and security".

In the global power game, the power to dispose of two types of resources is crucial for the economic performance of economies. These are the natural resources, as well as the human and technical productive resources. The focus can be different in the countries and nations. Countries and nations organize their respective economic systems differently, in order to achieve their economic production and economic results. For example, there are countries that rely more heavily on agriculture and natural resources. Other countries place greater emphasis on technical and scientific resources.

For a better understanding of the context, we must briefly put ourselves in the perspective of the elites of the United States, who have taken responsibility for the implementation

---

[21] In Wikipedia we find the following definition: *Tribute historically refers to a levy or tax. The tribute was paid as a sign of submission or vassal loyalty. As a rule, these were regular cash or non-cash benefits that were not only economically significant, but also expressed the balance of power.*

of the country strategy in pursuit of the purpose of achieving, steadily expanding, and further consolidating global hegemony. Within the framework of this short book, we can only present a sketch and a brief overview. Nevertheless, we intend to make it clear to the informed reader "where the journey is heading" and what the recognized goals and intentions of the USA are. We want to proceed in an evidence-based manner by providing hints to gain insights into the hidden motives and intentions by pointing out processes and connections.

At the strategic level, we see two essential factors or actors, on whose efforts and contributions the USA's striving for global hegemony is based. On the one hand, this is the military-economic complex, with companies such as Lockheed Martin, Raytheon Technologies, Boeing, Northrop Grumman, and on the other hand, these actors are the large financial cartels and global investment funds, such as Black Rock and the Capital Group, which now by far surpass the largest US banks in global importance[22].

The military-economic complex pursues two main goals. It strives for a steady increase in profits, and it also wants to continuously increase its potential to produce warlike weapons and military equipment. The military-economic complex achieves these goals via the American foreign and trade policy and by initiating and stirring up the maximum number of military conflicts globally on Earth and also in space[23], endeavoring to keep them running steadily. This creates the sales markets for the armaments and, if possible, expands them again and again. So the cynical proverb applies here: *war feeds its children*. The limit for this warmongering behavior is set, in the

---

[22] There are a large number of publications on these topics. In Germany, Werner Rügemer in particular has written excellent books and writings on the subject.

A study by the Hans Böckler Foundation also offers a good insight into the topic:
https://www.boeckler.de/de/boeckler-impuls-die-besitzer-der-welt-3512.htm.

[23] Tim Marschall has written the book "Geography of the Future", 2023, in which he shows "How the struggle for supremacy in space will change our world".

sense of game theory, by the fact that too many wars and conflicts would either exhaust countries and nations, or wipe out humanity as a whole. This has to be avoided. It is therefore important for the military-industrial complex and its representatives in the US government to manage the warlike "stories" in such a way that they are kept going all the time, but never go beyond a "sustainable" level. The war must not be allowed to "unwind". There must never be a standstill in this "game".

For the second important actor in the US strategy for global hegemony, i.e. for the big financial cartels and global investment funds[24], it is crucial to always be able to skim off a substantial part of the results of the global human and industrial production. The stream of revenues must flow continuously and, according to the iron law of capitalism, must steadily keep growing.[25] The military-economic complex has an important role to

---

[24] Formerly this was called "capital" in economics.

[25] In the USA, Noam Chomsky has presented the clearest analyses on this. But R. Buckminster Fuller also has good, clear descriptions of this, e.g. in "The Critical Path".

play in this, because it must ultimately ensure that, as far as possible, all countries on earth follow the "rules-based order" prescribed by American foreign policy. They must open up to Anglo-American capital and function economically in such a way that an optimum return is achieved.

If we keep these "conscious" intentions and goals of the responsible elites of the USA in mind and look at them in the reality of global events, as well as geopolitical and economic processes, then certain points become clear very quickly.

We know that the US maintains numerous military bases globally[26]. These do not serve to maintain peace, but they serve to initiate, keep going and constantly rekindle an optimum of conflicts in order to enable the military-industrial complex and the global financial cartels of the USA to achieve maximum results. These results are therefore of a financial, as well as of a military-technological nature. As a consequence, this

---

[26] For an overview of the military bases of the USA: https://de.wikipedia.org/wiki/Liste_von_Milit%C3%A4r basen_der_Vereinigten_Staaten_im_Ausland.

means that the financial cartels are behind and support the behavior and strategy of the US military-industrial complex, because they too can directly gain their advantages, i.e. make profits. One is tempted to call this a *synergetic management* within the framework of American hegemonic politics. In this way, new opportunities for profitable investments are constantly emerging, which can then be used for technological innovations by the industrial-military complex, the space industry and the American Tech giants. The profits generated by wars in turn generate the financial resources for more and more investment in more and more wars. In this way, the implementation of the strategy for global dominance by the USA serves both the military-industrial complex and the interests of the global Anglo-American financial cartels. The interests of the two are closely interwoven.[27] In other words, the financial

[27] A good overview of this topic is provided by Jeffry Sachs' essay on the "Agenda of US Foreign Policy", on December 20, 2023, on Telepolis: https://www.telepolis.de/features/Kriegsdebakel-und-viel-Geld-Die-geheime-Agenda-hinter-der-gescheiterten-US-Aussenpolitik-9584068.html?seite=all.

strength and economic system of the USA, as the basis for its global power, are essentially built on the coordinated strategic geopolitical actions of the military-industrial complex and the resources and investments of the financial cartels and banks, as the two supporting pillars.

In addition, the financial cartels also have an interest in ensuring that people in all countries and nations are as good consumers as possible and have a good income. So this interest also drives the global development of capitalism.[28] Through their participation in almost all sectors of the global economy and industry,[29] the sources of income for the Anglo-American financial cartels have nowadays become practically inexhaustible. The results and profits of the economic activities of people all over the globe always flow to a substantial extent directly to the Anglo-American financial cartels, be it in the

[28] This was the insight Ford gained during its early car production. The workers in the factories will also use part of their income to buy his cars, so a "win-win" situation.

[29] According to the cited study by the Hans Böckler Foundation, there is no DAX-listed company in which Black Rock does not have a stake.

form of financial revenues, be it in the constant expansion of the power of disposal and possession of the productive resources of countries and nations.

We would like to conclude these introductory explanations by briefly referring to the background of the current conflict between the USA and China, and by making comments on the war that is being waged against Russia in Ukraine.

Russia has relatively low economic output and productivity. However, it is the country on earth that owns the largest part of the natural resources and also has the technical skills to extract these resources and make them accessible to the global economy. It is therefore clear that the US will do everything, "whatever it takes", to have these resources at its disposal. This is the background to the current war in Ukraine and the constant fomenting of unrest in Europe and Central Asia. Europe is "rich" in manpower, i.e. in well-educated people and engineers. But its natural wealth is located in the Eurasian part of the continent.

China has with its people the greatest potential of common sense and intelligence in the world, coupled with the unique discipline and great diligence of the Chinese population.[30] The goal of the financial cartels is therefore to continuously skim off a certain part of the result of the productive performance of the people in China. Let's imagine that only 2 or 5% of China's economic output would flow to the USA and its financial cartels in a constantly flowing stream. Each of us will be able to understand that this is a fantastic dream for the owners and managers of Black Rock and their investors, the vision of a "Scrooge Duck", the American eager and lucky guy, who is always fortunate, and to whom money and wealth flow in a steady stream.

We would like to briefly point out here that we do not intend to go into detail here about the unconscious motives and motivations that control the US elites in the area of the military-industrial complex and the financial cartels. We know that many people in the USA believe that they have the task of

---

[30] A good insight into this is provided by "The Soul of China", 1925, Richard Wilhelm, as well as the various publications and books by Joseph Needham, such as "Moulds of Understanding", 1976.

making the world happy with their American way of life and their rules and order. The people on earth who do not belong to the American world of thought may not be able to understand this missionary vision of the USA. Unconsciously, however, it probably controls a good part of the behavior of the elites of the USA.[31] Other unconscious motives may also be at play. But we will not be able to go into this in detail in the context of the present study.[32]

---

[31] On the subject of "Manifest Destiny", i.e. the "obvious destiny" of the USA as the savior of the world, there are very good studies and books, all of which, directly or indirectly, support our argumentation. Mentioned here: Sam W. Hayes, Christopher Morris (eds.):Manifest Destiny and Empire: American Antebellum Expansionism, 1997; Reginald Horsman: Race and Manifest Destiny: The Origins of American Racial Anglo-Saxonism, 1981; Frederick Merk: Manifest Destiny and Mission in American History: A Reinterpretation, 1963; Anders Stephanson: Manifest Destiny: American Expansionism and the Empire of Right, 1995.

[32] Even in standard history books on the history of the USA, reference is made to this American self-image of the "chosen", special people. The History of the United States, 2nd Edition, 2013, by Allen C. Guelzo, et al.

In the following chapters, we will now at least briefly outline the scheme, according to which the United States acts militarily and economically in its international relations in the pursuit to achieve and consolidate its "strategic" intentions and goals in the struggle for global hegemony.

INTERDEPENDENCIES AND MAIN ELEMENTS OF THE MODEL OF AMERICAN HEGEMONY

In a brief overview, we want to present the connections and elements of the model of American hegemony schematically, in the form of a sketch, in order to make the actions and the underlying "logic" of the responsible elites of the military-industrial complex and the financial cartels of the USA understandable. If we consider that the U.S. hegemonic ambition is a global project that is also characterized by great dynamism, then we will understand why we will present this model only in a kind of sketch. We will concentrate on the essentials in order to show the basic functioning in an understandable way. It would certainly be interesting and worthy of the work of a research institute, or the research department of a foreign or defense ministry, to take such a sketch as a basis to build a comprehensive interactive computer-based model from it. Such a computer-based model would allow simulations of processes and of various scenarios based on a multitude of different and changing parameters. This would facilitate the virtual observation and understanding of a multitude of potential interactions of the most important actors, elements and factors to be watched in parallel on different screens. This would correspond to the model of a simulation of American foreign policy. We assume that such digitally controlled models have been set up at the Pentagon and the US State Department and are used for ongoing strategy development. We would call our sketch good, if it were sufficient as a starting point for such a model, i.e. if it showed the essential elements and most important parameters in context that could be understood in terms of system theory.

In building our basic model, we were guided by the following questions: From the perspective of the responsible elites of the USA, what are the most important elements, mechanisms, instruments and steps for the enforcement of US interests on a global level? What determines their actions? What is the strategic "logic" that guides everything and sets the framework for every action?

PRACTICAL GUIDE & THE LOGIC OF THE MODEL

So here is a short step-by-step summary of the[33] practice-oriented "guideline" we imagine for the responsible elites of the USA in the pursuit of global hegemony:

I.   Understand and determine your critical needs: identify the resources that can be useful in your relentless pursuit of the growth of your income, wealth, and power;

II.   In the different geopolitically important regions of the world, look for the partner(s), countries and nations that can best satisfy your needs for access and disposal of these resources;

III. Analyze the political dynamics in the region, in which these partners are

---

[33] This practice-oriented guideline is "imagined" by us. Based on our analyses and observation of the actual geopolitical sequences of events, we assume that it is realistic.

located, the interactions, connections, relationships and interdependencies;

IV.	The most important strategic tool you should use, when forming partnerships in the respective regions: create new and greater dependencies on the USA whenever possible: financially, technologically, ideologically, politically and legally;

a.	Possible ways and means to create such dependencies are:

i.	Bind your partners through contracts: this puts relations on a supposedly rules-based, high ethical level, perhaps even binding under international law, and gives credibility in the current political arena;

ii.	Create trade relations and buy goods from your partners: this builds trust and promotes mutual economic dependence;

iii. Make enemies for your partners[34]: this binds your partners closer to you because you are their friend and promise to help them fight against their enemies[35];

iv. Sell weapons to your partners to fight the enemies: this creates income for you and finances the military-economic complex, on which your own economy has become highly dependent. (see the economic structure of the USA and the UK, whose Keynesian economic model for both countries is now characterized by the dominance of the financial industry and the military-industrial complex. In

---

[34] In the toolboxes of the "regime change" actors as well as agencies, such as the CIA, there are certainly a whole lot of instruments that can be used effectively.
[35] A well-known example is the support of Sunni Wahhabi Saudi Arabia against its Shiite "enemies". The war between Iraq and Iran is also a good example of how wars are fueled by arms sales to both sides and "successfully" used for their own interests.

the case of the USA, there are also the tech giants and social media producers);[36]

v. Get paid for your weapons with the money you used to pay your regional partners for their goods and the resources that are important to you: this will lead to a return of funds to your own banks and financial cartels. The funds returned can then be reinvested. Profits from investments in the regions concerned are skimmed off at the same time;

---

[36] For a quick overview of the questions of economic structure, we recommend the website of Statista: https://de.statista.com/statistik/daten/. The study "The US Economy" in the information of the Federal Agency for Civic Education (bpb) of 20.03.2014 is also recommended. In the study by Prof. Dr. Juli Püschel in the bpb issue of 13.09.2021 on "Deindustrialization and High Tech in the USA" there are also interesting observations on our topic. Due to the current efforts to re-industrialize the USA in connection with the war in Ukraine, parts of this study have to be interpreted differently today.

vi. Support your partners with advice for investing the money, that remains with them after buying weapons and other goods with you, in your banks and financial institutions: this creates an even greater dependency, because your partners will eventually no longer be able to freely dispose of their own funds[37] and will increasingly learn to listen to you with confidence. In addition, it provides you with more and more financial potential and economic power;

vii. As a result, you will become the owner of your partners' resources. These resources can be "natural", such as oil and natural gas, but they can also consist of production and

---

[37] A current example from the years 2022-2024: as part of the current proxy war against Russia, Russia's assets abroad were "frozen" by the US and the EU and, contrary to international law, are being made available to Ukraine piece by piece for further warfare.

industrial capacities, as can be seen in the case of European countries, but also in the example of Japan and South Korea. In the language of Brzezinski, all these countries are "vassals" of the USA.

viii. It goes without saying that this model knows no boundaries. Inherent in this model is the "natural" capitalist urge for progress, eternal growth and constant expansion. In practice, the model therefore tends to spread across all countries and continents. In terms of the American "mission," we must understand the "happiness" that the U.S. wants to bring to all other nations in the world[38]. This guideline for the "pursuit of happiness" is also referring to

---

[38] We refer here again to our footnote to the "Manifest Destiny", i.e. the "obvious destiny" of the USA as the savior of the world, where relevant literature references can be found, all of which support our argumentation.

the strategic objectives inherent in the Monroe Doctrine and its successors, its details correspond to the policies proposed by Wilson in 1919, with his 14-point program and his proposal for the creation of the League of Nations, and the same guideline is still valid today with the Bretton Woods system of 1945, until our days.

If we have read and understood this brief overview of the "Praxeological Guide of the Responsible Elites of the USA", then we must acknowledge that the global policy of the USA has given itself a clear mandate and pursues clear goals. These are not laid down in the constitution. However, they correspond to the self-image of the USA, which has dedicated itself to the goal of the "pursuit of happiness", i.e. the pursuit of happiness in its own special American way, and which sees this happiness in the American way of life and in the worldwide shaping of societies and their relationships according to US rules and "values".

The most important negative element of this business model is that it is based on the production of weapons and armaments and on war as the decisive means of realizing profits. It is the business model of a global war economy.

We should also note that this "business model" of US global hegemonic and foreign policy only works really well on the condition that the other peoples, countries and nations actually seek their "happiness" in the same way, as it has become natural for the USA, and that they can therefore be subordinated to and subordinated to the business model as willing partners of the USA.

However, as soon as the other peoples, countries and nations align their happiness with other values and rules and do not want to integrate themselves into the "business model" of US global hegemonic and foreign policy, serious problems tend to arise. Then it usually soon comes to confrontation, or at least to sanctions and punishment. Then the USA resorts to the decisive and often forceful means within the framework of its economically, financially and militarily dominant power, usually with the blessing and under the umbrella of NATO and its members. Then the US and NATO take steps to launch "regime changes" through interventions, or direct military interventions, or wars of proxies, to help American power and its "privileged" partners[39] asserting and relentlessly pursuing their "legitimate" interests.

So at the moment when Russia resisted this model and, under Putin, increasingly withdrew national control over its own politics and resources from 2000 onwards, the contradiction with the US elites had become blatant, and a rift had been opened immediately that the US wanted to overcome by all means. This explains, why the hatred of the American elites is directed against Putin personally. We have to live with the results of these harmful emotions. The USA was determined to stage a war, if the "takeover" was not possible by peaceful means. After all, Russia is the country with the largest natural resources in the world, outside the North

---

[39] In the field of international politics, there is the concept of the "privileged partnership", which is used without a precise definition for supranational or intergovernmental relations.

American sphere, which is formed by Canada and the USA. These natural resources of Russia play a crucial role in the strategy of the United States in the struggle for global hegemony. The U.S. will not stop in their effort to take over these resources "at any cost," whatever the cost may be in human lives or in costs to the environment.

Russia did not accept the US peacefully getting the power to dispose of its natural resources, i.e. if it was not willing to accept the "price" that the USA offered them. By consequence, the USA has initiated a war in Ukraine and has driven the European countries and nations into this war against Russia. We will see more and more proxy wars in the future, because it makes other countries to pay and bear the burden. This is the situation we are experiencing with increasing intensity since the event of 9/11 in 2001. The situation we are living in is characterized by great dynamism, and has passed through many stations marked by violence and war, unto the current European war in Ukraine since 2022. These "experiences" are associated with high costs for the European "partners" of the USA.

Peaceful economic and political cooperation between the EU and Russia would certainly have been of greater benefit to European countries as a whole. However, the decisive prerequisite for this was missing. The EU and European countries have not found the will to shape their own destiny. The European elites and the people in Europe are paying a high price for the absence of courage and foresight, that have finally led to lack of sovereignty. This situation makes it also clear that the great time for Europe, in a process of historical erosion[40] since 1919, has finally come to a conclusion.

---

[40] The Risk Management Network published a very interesting article on October 7, 2019: "New Era of Great Power Conflicts – Erosion Processes of the Geopolitical World".
https://www.risknet.de/themen/risknews/erosionsproz esse-der-geopolitischen-welt/.

The strategic spheres of influence: the geopolitical world view of the USA

In the following, we present a first draft overview of the division of strategic geopolitical spheres of influence from a US perspective. We would like to refer at least briefly to the geopolitical concept of Nicholas J. Spykman[41], which he presented as early as 1938, and in which he pointed out the importance of the "*borderlands*[42]". Spykman writes "he who controls the surrounding countries rules Eurasia, he who rules Eurasia controls the fate of the world". Looking at the situation in Ukraine with the war against Russia, we can understand very well that the US is still today following this strategic

---

[41] see "Geography and Foreign Policy," by Nicholas J. Spykman, The American Political Science Review, Vol. XXXII, Nos. 1 and 2, February and April 1938.

[42] A recent book on this topic "Frontline Ukraine: Crisis in the Borderlands", 2022, Richard Sakwa.

concept and applying the inherent recommendation. [43]

We are aware that our overview can only provide a first approach. Our succinct document would have to be elaborated and refined in detail by a team of geopolitical and military strategists and continuously improved on the basis of new data. The world and the geopolitical facts are in constant evolution. We also see that the demarcation of the individual spheres of influence and empires cannot always be made unambiguously. The transitions between the individual geographical spheres are often fluid. However, the large, global connections should nevertheless become clear in our structured overview. The more detailed elaboration of this overview would have to be worked out by suitable institutes or universities using computer-assisted models. We assume that such simulation models

---

[43] A similar concept comes from Zbigniew Brzezinski, on "The Only World Power: America's Strategy of Dominance", 1999.
We also recommend the exciting reading of Anna Reid's book "Borderland, A Journey Through the History of the Ukraine", 2015.

already exist in the ministries of defense and foreign policy of the major nations.

For our argumentation, however, it is crucial to identify the parameters and rules for the functioning and as well as for the mechanisms and processes of the model and to present them in the appropriate context and in a coherent way. Only then can the model offer "realistic" scenarios that can then be recognized as guidelines for the individual actors.

We can assume that most individual actors are aware of the role they play on the geopolitical "chessboard" of the USA. Some may be satisfied with their role, while others may see themselves pushed into the role of "enemies". They all will strive to position themselves successfully to achieve their own goals and to take advantage through their actions, managing the processes and working on procedures as good as they can. This should at least be their intention, but it will require consciousness of the specific position and role, each one of the actors is occupying. Many of the participants will consider themselves autonomous actors and will believe that they act "of their own free will" and according to their own purpose and interests[44]. This book is written in particular for those actors, who are still under illusions. It is intended to show them that they are only pawns in a great geopolitical chess game[45], often with high stakes and a bloody outcome. They do not realize that they obey rules that are given by others.

At this point, we would like to refer once again to Gregory Bateson, who warns us in his writing about cybernetics that any understanding can be creative, but also "used destructively".[46] However, he insists that the

---

[44] The reference of this model to analytical individual psychology will not escape the attention of the educated reader.

[45] Mephistopheles already saw through these "games" well, and Goethe puts the following words into his mouth in his Faust II: Oh dear! away! and leave aside those quarrels, Of tyranny and slavery. I'm bored; for no sooner is it done, than they begin again; And no one notices: he is only teased, Of the Asmodeus who is behind it. They are fighting, it is said, about civil liberties, strictly speaking, they are servants against servants.

[46] This and the following quotations are taken from the lecture of 1966 "From Versailles to Cybernetics", published in Ecology of the Mind, page 603 ff., 1971.

"rules of the game" that are given to the computer for simulation are decisive for the result. If you confirm and accept the results of such a simulation, then you have "confirmed the rules of this game". From the perspective of cybernetics and system analysis, Gregory Bateson then gives us to consider "that there are some things that are wrong at the international level, that's why rules have to be changed".

In the concluding third part of this book, we will bring examples to demonstrate the possibility of changing the rules, by which we have been shaping our "models" of the world for the past five hundred centuries. We will show that such a change of rules is possible in different areas, and from our point of view also desirable and necessary. Using the example of the geopolitical strategy of the USA and its intention for global hegemony, we have been able to show, which basic rules are applied to manage and run the geopolitical business model of the USA, and according to which mechanisms it functions in practice.

In the concluding part of our book "Europe on the Way to Her Apocalypse" (2024), we are proposing and showing how rules can be changed in order to initiate paradigm shifts and also implement them in practice. There are convincing examples of this in politics and social life at the international level. We will refer to them. So we agree with Gregory Bateson when he says that "cybernetics itself contains the integrity that helps us not to be seduced by it into another madness". In the concluding part of the book, therefore, we join this view, consciously appreciating "that in cybernetics the means are also laid out... to change our philosophy of power...".

We do not want to pass over the opportunity to refer to an essay by Arnold J. Toynbee from 1934 that supports our argumentation. In the essay "Things Not Foreseen at Paris. The Future in Retrospect", Toynbee writes, referring to the negotiations for the Treaty of Versailles between statesmen, who established this "peace agreement" under an "outrageously naïve assumption". Then he concedes to these statesmen that they "could hardly be expected to foresee the resurgence of Turkey and China and Mexico and Russia and the other countries of the world that possessed ancient civilizations of non-

Western order. The Paris Peace Conference of 1919–1920 assumed that all non-Western countries, such as the defeated Western country of Germany, were at the disposal of the victorious Allied and Associated Powers, with whom they could deal as they pleased, and because the control and exploitation of the Asian and African, Indonesian and Antillean dominions was both feasible and profitable for the Western powers during the 18th and 19th centuries." Toynbee then concludes his essay with a warning by pointing out that "our problem is to complete our education, and we cannot do it calmly, because time is the essence of the problem we face. It seems to be a race between belated wisdom and premature death by suicide."

As we have seen in our analysis and presentation so far, in our current contemporary history we are still dealing with a model that obviously follows the rules that guided the negotiations on the Treaty of Versailles some hundred years ago. The rules and mechanisms inherent to this model have shaped the "patterns of our relations" in international politics since then and up to the present time. Our overview has served the purpose of providing the reader with the clearest possible overview of the global strategic approach of the USA to assert and consolidate its hegemonic interests in line with this model. We were also able to summarize some of the results the USA has "achieved" in the past century, especially in the last 50 years. We could then show how the USA has designed its business model and with clever strategic thrust put it into practice in emphatical pursuit of its interests and to achieve its goals.

As we have seen, the primary interest of the United States, globally, is to secure and expand hegemonic dominance on Earth. The means, by which this overarching strategic goal is to be achieved, are the securing and expansion of the military presence and dominance, the increase in political power, which is to be achieved primarily through the financial dominance of the Anglo-American-dominated financial cartels, and the ever-increasing cultural dominance and improved control by the American culture industry and social media.[47]

This overview has also been able to make it clear that the current wars did not arise by chance. Their creation follows rules and patterns, which we were able to summarize on the basis of the sketch of the business model and the summary of the strategic "guideline". Our analytical presentation and overview has also already indicated that the "hot spots" that are actively promoted and shaped by the USA are regionally divided according to geopolitical spheres. We also pointed out the basic rules that are responsible for ensuring that all these tensions, conflicts and wars practically never end. They have no expiration date and at best shift to neighboring areas or states, but often they spread out, as we can see well from the example of the "Arab Spring" since 2010. From "rebellions" to civil wars and finally also to wars, if we want to take Syria and Libya into account. In addition, all this has resulted in large movements of refugees, as unintended negative collateral consequences

---

[47] In Brzezinski's "Chess board" these points are clearly presented.

[48], which no longer want to subside and can no longer be contained.

Our view on this shocking scenario implicitly warns against assuming that these conflicts and wars have arisen by chance and will come to an end. Rather, based on our analytical overview, we should understand by now that this aggressive and unrelenting US approach is at the core of its geopolitical quest for global hegemony.

The characteristics of the USA's hegemonic striving and the respective procedure to achieve the strategic goals still apply, even if the USA has these conflicts and wars waged essentially by proxy, through so-called "proxy wars". There are many clear examples that provide evidence of this. We only want to mention the various wars of Saudi Arabia against Iran, the war against Russia by Ukraine, which is being waged with the active participation of Germany, Great Britain,

---

[48] In the social sciences and humanities, the principle of "unintended consequences" or "unintended effects" has been known for a long time.
https://de.wikipedia.org/wiki/Unbeabsichtigte_Folgen#cite_note-1.

France, Poland and other European NATO countries, as well as the current conflict over Taiwan, in which Japan and South Korea are positioning themselves militarily as essential proxies of the USA.

It should also be clear that this business model develops in a dynamic global environment. Actors change their behavior, or reposition themselves. Things and circumstances are constantly changing, be it military-technical, geopolitical, scientific and technological. Just think of the modern drone wars, the prerequisites for which were created during the administration of US President Barack Obama and US Secretary of State Hilary Clinton and also "tested" in practice during the occupation of Afghanistan. New weapon systems are constantly being developed. The role of reconnaissance satellites and the creation of cyber space and cyber war capabilities are other important examples. In the 19th century, no one had cyberspace in its current form in mind. Geopolitically, no one could know or foresee with certainty how Russia would develop after the October Revolution, or how the political and economic development of China, India and Pakistan would proceed in the 20th century. One hundred years ago, no one could have foreseen the age of computers and the Internet, or artificial intelligence. So new circumstances are constantly being created, to which the US strategy will adapt, to which it must find the appropriate answers, if it wants to be successful in its specific sense. However, we must not make the mistake of confusing such adaptations to new circumstances with changing the rules of the game. Our analytical description should have made it clear by now that the basic rules, according to which the American geopolitical business model works, have remained the same to this day.

The following structured overview will also make one thing clear to us: if there is no fundamental change in the attitude that the main players of the business model obey, and the most important actors here are certainly the US elites, then this hegemonic striving for power by the USA will continue to cause many conflicts, civil wars and wars. So we should not be under any illusions in this regard.

In order for humanity to win this "race between belated wisdom and premature death by suicide", of which Toynbee writes in his essay, a necessary mental change[49], a fundamental renewal of the psychic equipment[50], as well as the courage and insight into the necessity to change the rules of geopolitics that guide international relations are necessary.

When we ask ourselves how this spiral of violence and wars can be ended and what we as humanity can do to make the earth a place, where there will be room for more peace and understanding, we agree that there are no easy answers. This behavior seems to be too deeply ingrained in the human psyche, which seems to give priority to the pursuit of power and wealth at all costs over all other values.

The first important step, however, is to create awareness of the situation. We want to serve

---

[49] Karen Armstrong also speaks of the necessity of an intellectual renewal in the introduction to her book on the "Axial Age", i.e. the Axial Age of the great civilizations
[50] Reference should be made here to the psychological essay by C. G. Jung from 1933, Modern Men in Search of a Soul, in German "Modern Man in Search of a Soul".

this purpose and therefore continue with our overview and analytical presentation.

STRUCTURED OVERVIEW:
THE GEOPOLITICAL SPHERES OF INFLUENCE

The most important structuring factor in U.S. geopolitical strategy are, how could it be otherwise for a nation as "goal-oriented" and pragmatic as the U.S.,

the key industries [51] (according to the Brzeziński Doctrine):

> ➤ military-industrial complex;

> ➤ financial industry;

> ➤ Culture Industry.

For the following structured overview on the geopolitical spheres of influence, we refer to ongoing international discussions and studies. We provide appropriate information and references in each case. There is broad international consensus on this "structure of empires" and nothing is invented by us or drawn out of our own thinking only. In English-language literature, the term

---

[51] In American English, unlike in German, "industries" are everything that concerns economic activity, i.e. that can yield profits and help generate income.

"empire" is often used for these geopolitical spheres of influence. We refer her in particular to the British historian Niall Ferguson and follow his practice in our structured overview, therefore speaking of strategic "empires".

The strategic spheres of empires are structured as shown on the pages to follow:

A   Europe[52]

Strategic   partners: West-Central-South-Central Europe;

Coveted booty: Russia, with its natural resources and its singular strategic geopolitical location stretching over the Eurasian continent;

Thorn in the flesh: Ukraine, the Baltic States, Georgia, Moldova;

---

[52] In Europe, contemporary research on these global contexts and processes of "power and money" has largely fallen silent, adapted to the mainstream, or allowed itself to be pushed to the margins of society. For example, German trade unions are discussing whether a war economy can make sense because it creates new jobs. There are pleasing exceptions to such currents, especially in England, e.g. by Niall Ferguson.

<u>Primary resources:</u> industry, technology, know-how;

<u>Main wars, civil wars, armed conflicts</u>:

WW1, WW2, "Cold" War, Turkey vs. Greece, Cyprus, Yugoslavia, Ukraine;

<u>Main US military bases + allies (incl. NATO)</u>: Germany, Italy, Spain, Poland, Romania, Hungary, Czech Republic, Kosovo;

B   Middle East[53]

<u>Strategic partners:</u> Saudi Arabia, Egypt, Jordan, Morocco, Turkey (Ottoman Empire);

<u>Coveted booty:</u> Iran, Iraq, Syria, Arabian Peninsula;

<u>Thorn in the flesh:</u> Israel;

---

[53] In the context of studies on the role of oil in economic development since the rapid industrialization of Europe in the 20th century, the topics of political and economic power are also frequently discussed. Scholarly research on these connections has led to an increasingly independent political discussion and position, especially on the development of the Muslim Brotherhood, especially in Egypt, but today also in other countries and states (Turkey, Algeria, Jordan).

Primary resources: crude oil, natural gas;

Most important wars, civil wars, armed conflicts: Israel vs. Palestine, Iran, Iraq, Yemen, Libya, Syria;

Main US military bases + allies (incl. NATO): Saudi Arabia, UAE, Israel, Djibouti, Iraq;

C East Asia - Far East[54]

Strategic partners: Japan, Korea, Philippines;

Coveted booty: China;

Thorn in the flesh: Taiwan (Chinese nationalists), North-South Korea;

Primary resources: primarily human-intellectual resources, markets;

---

[54] In what his opponents call the "Chinese dictatorship", the richest intellectual life of all the countries on earth is probably flourishing and stirring at the moment. There is a spirit of optimism in China. In the broader and deeper context of ZHAO Tingyang's studies on what the Chinese call "Tianxia", *the most interesting and fruitful discussions of ideas and scientific thoughts are currently taking place on* the topic of the "future of world order" (global governance) in an open and creative atmosphere.

<u>Main wars, civil wars, armed conflicts</u>: Japan vs. Russia, Japan vs. China, Civil War China (Nationalists vs. Communists), Vietnam, Korea, Philippines vs. China, India vs. China, Indonesia (Civil War);

<u>Main US military bases + allies (incl. NATO)</u>: Guam, Japan, South Korea, Philippines;

D   South and Southeast Asia[55]

<u>Strategic partners:</u> Australia, India, Pakistan, Philippines, Thailand, Singapore;

---

[55] There is a lively scientific and political discussion about this "strategic empire" and correspondingly a large number of very good studies and books, especially from India and Pakistan. There are no topics that are not dealt with intensively and in high-quality discourses. This sphere of influence offers a very good example of the complexity of geopolitical contexts and the resulting challenges for people and their communities of states to find their way to a prosperous and peaceful coexistence. Nowhere is it more evident than in this part of the world that man must rise above his present spiritual state if he wants to make his future life on planet Earth good and prosperous. Within the framework of the existing mechanisms and under the application of the previous rules, the dynamics of violence and war will not diminish.

<u>Coveted booty:</u> Indian Ocean, Strait of Malacca, South Pacific;

<u>Thorn in the flesh:</u> Pakistan, Myanmar, Vietnam;

<u>Primary resources:</u> multiple natural and human-intellectual resources;

<u>Main wars, civil wars, armed conflicts:</u>

Vietnam, Korea, Philippines vs. China, India vs. China, India vs. Pakistan, Indonesia (Civil War);

<u>Main US military bases + allies (new: AUKUS):</u> Australia, Philippines, Thailand;

E   **Central Asia**[56]

<u>Strategic partners:</u> Kazakhstan, Turkmenistan, Turkey (Ottoman Empire);

<u>Coveted prey:</u> Bactria (Afghanistan, Tajikistan, Uzbekistan), according to

---

[56] This "strategic empire" is characterized by the fact that it is located in the geopolitical center, surrounded by the great Euro-Asian states and powers, currently India, China, Russia, EU, Persia. This probably also corresponds to his global-historical role (see "Foundations of Eastern Civilization" by Craig G. Benjamin).

Mackinder theory[57] the "heartland" for global dominance;

<u>Thorn in the flesh:</u> Armenia, Georgia, Azerbaijan;

<u>Primary resources:</u> multiple, mainly natural resources, strategic platform (global "heartland");

<u>Main wars, civil wars, armed conflicts:</u> Afghanistan, Armenia vs. Azerbaijan (Nagorno-Karabakh), Georgia (Ossetia, Abkhazia), Tajikistan vs. Kyrgyzstan;

<u>Main US military bases + allies (incl. NATO):</u> Turkey, Georgia, Pakistan, NATO partner countries in Central Asia (Kazakhstan,

---

[57] Halford Mackinder, a British geographer, published the article "The Geographical Pivot of History" in 1904, in which he redefined the understanding of space and power in international politics. His "Heartland Theory" had a significant impact on British geopolitics and has since played an important role in global governance, i.e. the structure of world power.
"The Geographical Pivot of History" is an article submitted by Halford John Mackinder to the Royal Geographical Society in 1904, which further develops his theory of the heartland. In this article, Mackinder expanded the scope of geopolitical analysis to cover the entire globe

Kyrgyzstan, Tajikistan, Turkmenistan, Uzbekistan);

F   America: North-Central-South[58]

Strategic partners: Brazil, Canada, Chile;

Coveted prey: general U.S. dominance (Monroe Doctrine & Successors);

Thorn in the flesh: Cuba, Colombia, Peru;

Primary resources: multiple, mainly natural resources, markets;

Main wars, civil wars, armed conflicts:

USA vs. Mexico + a multitude of wars between the South American states, plus a multitude of "interventions", "overthrows" and "regime changes" that were initiated and promoted by the U.S. to "preserve its own security". It is generally recognized that the CIA is playing an active role and interventions are often carried out under the direction of the CIA.

---

[58] Research and discussions in North and South America are lively and intensive, and often of high quality, at universities and institutes. The influence of this research is determined by the elites.

<u>Main US military bases + allies (incl. NATO):</u> SOUTHCOM – US facility to organize the regional military presence (currently about 76 military bases on the Latin American sub-continent and the Caribbean, divided into 3 categories: base of operations; small military base; US-funded base.

G   Black Africa (Sub-Saharan Africa)[59]

<u>Strategic partners:</u> South Africa, Botswana, Namibia, Ivory Coast, Cameroon, Kenya, Chad;

---

[59] The most important research on Africa's role in the global context of geopolitical discussions is still carried out by African-Americans and Africans outside Africa. This is mainly due to the modest resources of African institutes and universities. Nevertheless, there is a lively and often well-founded discussion among large parts of the African elites in Africa. So there is no lack of understanding of the connections. But there is a lack of assertiveness of the results of research on the question of Africa's future positioning in global political and economic interaction. Symptomatic of the situation is the "Africa Institute" in the Arab Emirates (UAE), which has virtually no influence on the discussions in Africa and does not want to move its headquarters to Africa.

Coveted prey: primarily the Congo Basin, oil in Angola, Gabon, Congo, Nigeria;

Thorn in the flesh: apartheid, legacy of slavery;

Primary resources: multiple, mainly natural resources;

Main wars, civil wars, armed conflicts: Angola, Congo, Rwanda, Ethiopia, Sudan, South Africa/South Africa (anti-apartheid), Chad, Somalia;

Main US military bases + allies (incl. NATO): Diego Garcia, Kenya, Djibouti (France + USA), Senegal (through France), Niger (drone base until 2024), USA Africa Command (based in Stuttgart, Germany);

BIBLIOGRAPHY

Abelshauser, Werner; Wunder gibt es immer wieder: Mythos Wirtschaftswunder, in: Aus Politik und Zeitgeschichte, 68 (2018) 27, S. 4-10.

Ansprenger, Franz; Auflösung der Kolonialreiche, 1989.

Armstrong, Karen; The Great Transformation: The Axial Age, 2005. Deutsch: Achsenzeit der grossen Zivilisationen, 2006.

Attali, Jacques; Biographie: C'était François Mitterand, Paris, 2007.

Bateson, Gregory; Geist und Natur. Eine notwendige Einheit, 1987.

Bateson, Gregory; in Ökologie des Geistes, Teil VI, Krisen in der Ökologie des Geistes, von Versailles zur Kybernetik, Vorlesung von 1966.

Bateson, Gregory; Ökologie des Geistes, 1985; English edition: Steps to an Ecology of Mind, Collected Essays, 1972.

Bell, Daniel A, Amitav Acharya, Rajeev Bhargava, Yan Xuetong (eds.); Bridging two Worlds, Comparing Classical Political Thought and Statecraft in India and China, 2003. University of California Press, series: Great Transformations.

Benjamin, Craig G.; Foundations of Eastern Civilization,

Berger, Jens; Wer schützt die Welt vor den Finanzkonzernen?, Frankfurt, 2020.

Bernstein, Richard J.; Beyond objectivism and relativism: Science, Hermeneutics, and Praxis, University of Pennsylvania Press 1983.

Bittner, Wolfgang; Die Eroberung Europas durch die USA, 2015.

Blankart, Charles B.; Föderalismus in Deutschland und in Europa, 2007, erschienen in der Reihe „Neue Studien zur Politischen Ökonomie", Nomos Verlag.

Blankart, Charles B.; Öffentliche Finanzen in der Demokratie: Eine Einführung in die Finanzwissenschaft, Gebundene Ausgabe, 2017.

Bloch, Marc; Die Feudalgesellschaft, Neuausgabe 2019, Französisches Original von 1939.

Bono, Edward de; Lateral Thinking: a Textbook of Creativity, 1970.

Bono, Edward de; Laterales Denken : Ein Kursbuch zur Erschliessung ihrer Kreativitätsreserven, 1971.

Bördlein, Christoph; Einführung in die Verhaltensanalyse (English edition: Introduction to Behavioral Analysis), 2015.

Born, Max; Der Mensch und das Atom, in: Ausblick auf die Zukunft, 1968.

Bozo, Frederic; Deux stratégies pour l'Europe, Paris, 1996.

Bracher, Andreas; Europa im amerikanischen Weltsystem, Bruchstücke zu einer ungeschriebenen Geschichte des 20. Jahrhunderts, 2001.

Bracher, Andreas; Völkische Selbstbestimmung und Dreigliederung, in der Zeitschrift Perseus, der Europäer, Jg. 6 Nr. 8, Juni 2002.

Brandt, Willy; Frieden sichern und Mauern überwinden – Ost- und Deutschlandpolitik 1955–1989. https://www.willy-brandt-biografie.de/politik/ost-und-deutschlandpolitik/

Braudel, Fernand; Die lange Dauer. in: Schriften zur Geschichte, Bd. 1: Gesellschaft und Zeitstrukturen. 1992, S. 49–87. Ganz wichtig in unserem Zusammenhang ist „Die Geschichte der Zivilisation vom 15 bis zum 18 Jahrhundert, 1982.

Braudel, Fernand; Histoire et Sciences sociales : La longue durée, in : Annales, Année 1958, pp. 725-753.

Braudel, Fernand; L'Identité de la France, auf Deutsch herausgegeben als «Frankreich, Band 1: Raum und Geschichte / Band 2: Die Menschen und die Dinge / Band 3: die Dinge und die Menschen, 2009.

Braudel, Fernand; La dynamique du capitalisme. Paris, 1985. Deutsch als: Die Dynamik des Kapitalismus, 1991.

Braun, Eduard; Pseudoliberale Staatsinterventionen und die Neoklassik . Gedanken zum Homo Oeconomicus und zum wahren Wert der Dinge, Mises Institute, Mises Wire, 11. April 2022.

Bricker, Darrell and Ibbitson, John; Empty Planet: The Shock of Global Population Decline, 2019

Briggs, John und Peat, F. David; Die Entdeckung des Chaos, 1997; das Original ist 1989 unter dem Titel „Turbulent Mirror" in New York veröffentlicht worden.

Brzezinski, Zbigniew, The Grand Chessboard: American Primacy and its Geostrategic Imperatives, 1997.

Brzezinski, Zbigniew; Die einzige Weltmacht: Amerikas Strategie der Vorherrschaft, 1999.

Burkhard, Jakob; Kultur der Renaissance in Italien, Erstveröffentlichung 1860.

Butterwegge, Christoph; Die zerrissene Republik. Wirtschaftliche, soziale und politische Ungleichheit in Deutschland, 2019.

Campbell, Joseph; Thou art That. Transforming Religious Metaphor. The spiritual meaning of Biblical Stories, Miracles and Parables, 2002.

Campbell, Joseph; Understanding and Interpretation of Mythology. The Website of the Joseph Campbell Foundation: https://www.jcf.org/.

Fritjof; Tao der Physik, 1977.

Carstens, Peter; Deutsch-Französisches Projekt: Ein Kampfflugzeug für 100 Milliarden Euro, in der FAZ vom 21.01.2020.

Carter, Robert; Frank Lloyd Wright, A Biography, 2006.

Chomsky, Noam; Sprache und Geist, 1970. Darin der Anhang aus *New Left Review* (Nummer 57, September/Oktober 1969).

Chomsky, Noam; Rules and Representations. Behavioral and Brain Sciences, 1980. . Deutsch: Regeln und Repräsentationen, 1980

Chomsky, Noam; Gespräch mit C. J. Polychroniou zum Thema „Warum China, nicht Russland die US-dominierte Weltordnung bedroht", auf Deutsch am 09.07.2022 in Telepolis; Original in Trouthout.

Chomsky, Noam; in Asia-Pacific-Forum vom 31.12.2012, Revenge Of History: Chomsky on Japan, China, The United States, And The Threat of Conflict in Asia".

Clark, Christopher; Die Schlafwandler: Wie Europa in den Ersten Weltkrieg zog, 2013.

Clark, Christopher; Von Zeit und Macht, 2918.

Club of Rome, Grenzen des Wachstums, 1962.

Couvée, Leonard; Verslumung als Folge von Metropolisierung, 2016.

Covey, Stephen R.; Die 7 Wege zur Effektivität, Original von 1990, deutsch 1996.

Dagdelen, Sevim; Die NATO: Eine Abrechnung mit dem Wertebündnis, 2024.

Dangeleit, Elke; Deutschland finanziert Erdogans Umsiedelungspolitik in Nord- und Ostsyrien, Online Magazin Telepolis, vom 24. Januar 2020.

Davis, Irvine Mike; Planet der Slums, Department of History an der University of California, 2005; Planet der Slums ist 2019 auf Deutsch erschienen.

Denson, John V.; "A Century of War" wurde 1997 als Vortrag zum fünfzehnjährigen Jubiläum des Ludwig von Mises Institute gehalten und Mises.org veröffentlicht.

Desjardins, T. ; François Mitterand: un socialiste gaullien, Paris, 1978.

Diamond, Jared; Guns, Germs and Steel. The Fates of Human Societies, 1998.

Doering-Manteuffel, Anselm; Amerikanisierung und Westernisierung, Version: 2.0, in: Docupedia-Zeitgeschichte, 19.08.2019.

Dresdener gesammelte Kommentare zur Sicherheitspolitik – dgksp-diskussionspapiere – vom 14. April 2021.

Duerr, Hans-Peter; Der Mythos vom Zivilisationsprozeß, 2005.

Conze, Eckart; Hegemonie durch Integration: Die amerikanische Europapolitik und ihre Herausforderung durch de Gaulle, in: Institut für Zeitgeschichte, Vierteljahreshefte für Zeitgeschichte, Jahrgang 43 (1995), Heft 2.

Egli, Rene; Das Lola Prinzip, Die Vollkommenheit der Welt, 1994.

Ehrlich, Paul R.; The Population Bomb, New York: Ballantine Books 1968; dt. Übers.: Die Bevölkerungsbombe, 1971.

Eksteins, Modris; Rites of Spring: The Great War and the Birth of the Modern Age, 1989.

Evans, Richard; The Pursuit of Power, Europe 1815-1914, 2016.

Ferguson, Niall; Colossus: The Rise and Fall of the American Empire, 2004.

Ferguson, Niall; Eine Nation ist kein Individuum, und ein Individuum ist keine Nation, am 31.12.2021 in der NZZ.

Ferguson, Niall; Empire: How Britain Made the Modern World, 2003.

Ferguson, Niall; The Ascent of Money: A Financial History of the World, 2008.

Ferguson, Niall; The Cash Nexus. Money and Power in the Modern World, 1700–2000, 2001.

Ferguson, Niall; The War of the World: History's Age of Hatred, 1st Edition, 2009.

Fix, Andrew C.; The Renaissance, the Reformation and the Rise of Nations", Audible Audiobook series: „The Great Courses" produced by „The Teaching Company", 2005.

Focus Magazin Nr. 8, 2009; "Alles schon gelaufen?", Wem gehört Deutschland?

Foreign Affairs, Volume 103 Number 3, No Substitute for Victory, 2024. https://www.foreignaffairs.com/united-states/no-substitute-victory-pottinger-gallagher

Fortes, Meyer; The Political Systems of the Tallensi of the Northern Territories of the Gold Coast, in African Political Systems, M. Fortes and E.E. Evans-Pritchard (eds.), First Edition 1940.

Frankopan, Peter; The Silk Roads, The New History of the World, 2015.

Freud, Sigmund; Vorlesungen zur Einführung in die Psychoanalyse, 1917.

Friedrich, Marc und Weik, Matthias ; Komplette, legale Enteignung per Gesetz, 2019.

Fröhlich, Stefan; Die transatlantischen Beziehungen, Deutschland, 2017.

Fuller, R. Buckminster; Critical Path, 1981;

Fuller, R. Buckminster; Ideas and Integrities, 1963.

Fuller, R. Buckminster; Nine Chains to the Moon", 1938.

Fuller, R. Buckminster; Operating Manual for Spaceship Erath, 1969; deutsche Ausgabe: Bedienungsanleitung für das Raumschiff Erde und andere Schriften", 2011.

Gluckman, Max; The Limits of Naivety in Social Anthropology", 2017.

Goethe, J. W.; Faust, Tragödie Erster und Zweiter Teil, 1986.

Granet, Marcel; Die chinesische Zivilisation. Band 2: Das chinesische Denken. Inhalt, Form, Charakter, Ersterscheinung deutsch 1985. Original: „La pensée chinoise", Paris 1938.

Greene, Robert; Die Gesetze der menschlichen Natur, 2019; das englische Original „The Laws of Human Nature, 2018.

Greene, Robert; Gesetze der Macht. engl. The Laws of Power, 1998.

Grenoble University, Ecole de Management (GEM) de Grenoble, Energie for Society, Université de Grenoble, Politiques énergétiques : comment éviter une dystopie européenne?, 2024.
Griffin, George Edward; The Creature from Jekyll Island, 1994.

Grün, Arno; Dem Leben entfremdet, 2019.

Guelzo, Allen C., et al.; The History of the United States, 2003, 2nd Edition, 2013.

Guilford, J. P.; The Structure of Intellect, in Psychological Bulletin, Volume 53 N° 4, July 1956.

Habermas, Jürgen; Theorie des kommunikativen Handelns, 1981.

Hahn, Robert; Herrschaft von Lissabon bis Wladiwostok", 06.07.2022.

Hayek Friedrich A. v.; Weltwirtschaftliches Archiv, 36. Bd., 1932.

Hayes, Sam W. and Morris, Christopher (eds.): Manifest Destiny and Empire: American Antebellum Expansionism, 1997. Heer, Burkhard; Umwelt, Bevölkerungsdruck und Wirtschaftswachstum in Entwicklungsländern, 2013.

Hegel G.W.F.; Tagebuch der Reise in die Berner Oberalpen, 1796. In: K. Rosenkranz, G.W.F. Hegels Leben [1844]. Darmstadt 1969: 470–89.

Heinsohn, Gunnar; Söhne und Weltmacht, 1. Auflage 2005.

Heisterkamp, Jens (Hg.); Die Jahrhundertillusion. Wilsons Selbstbestimmungsrecht der Völker, Sammelband, 2002.

Hellmann, Gunther; Zwischen Gestaltungsmacht und Hegemoniefalle: Zur neuesten Debatte über eine neue deutsche Außenpolitik, in der Reihe „Aus Politik und Zeitgeschichte, 11.07.2016.

Heylighen, Francis; , Accelerating Evolution, 2007, in Modelski, Tessaleno and Thompson, William (eds.), "Globalization as an Evolutionary Process: Modeling Global Change", Rethinking Globalizations, London 2007.

Hobsbawm, Eric; Zeitalter der Extreme, Weltgeschichte des 20. Jahrhunderts, 1995.

Horkheimer, Max und Adorno, Theodor W.; Dialektik der Aufklärung, 1944.

Horsman, Reginald; Race and Manifest Destiny: The Origins of American Racial Anglo-Saxonism, 1981.

Hülsmann, Jörg Guido; Abundance, Generosity, and the State: an Inquiry into Economic Principles, 2024.

Hummel, Diana; Der Bevölkerungsdiskurs: Demographisches Wissen und politische Macht, 2000.

Hungary Today, Online Magazin vom 24. Mai 2024.

Hürter, Thomas; Das Zeitalter der Unschärfe, 2021.

Jordan, Pascual; Wie sieht die Welt von morgen aus?, 1958.

Jung, C. G.; Biographie: Erinnerungen, Träume, Gedanken, 1962.

Jung, C. G.; Modern Men in Search of a Soul", auf Deutsch „Der moderne Mensch auf der Suche nach einer Seele", von 1933.

Keynes, John Maynard; Krieg und Frieden: Die wirtschaftlichen Folgen des Vertrags von Versailles, 1920.

Koestler, Arthur and Smythies, J. R. (eds); Revolutionizing the Sciences of Man, 1968.

Koestler, Arthur; Jenseits von Atomismus und Holismus – Der Begriff des Holons, in, "Das Neue Menschenbild – Die Revolutionierung der Wissenschaften vom Menschen", 1970, Hrsg. Arthur Koestler und J. R. Smythies.

Kohlenberg, Kerstin und Schieritz, Mark; am 23. Oktober 2014, in DIE ZEIT Nr. 44/2014, Die Superwaffe des Mr. Glaser, Sanktionen gegen Russland und den Iran: Wie amerikanische Finanzbeamte zu Wirtschaftskriegern werden.

Konersmann, Ralf (Hrsg.); Kulturkritik: Reflexionen in der veränderten Welt, Reclam 2001.

Konicz, Tomasz; Türkei: Merkels zivilisatorischer Tabubruch, Online Magazin Telepolis, vom 25. Januar 2020.

Koselleck, Reinhard; Vergangene Zukunft. Zur Semantik geschichtlicher Zeiten, 1989.

Kreitner, R. & Kinicki, A; Organizational Behavior, 2004, New York: McGraw-Hill.

Krohne, Heinz W.; Psychologie der Angst, 2010.

Kuhn, Thomas S.; The Structure of Scientific Revolutions, 1962.

Lau, Jörg; "Regelbasierte Weltordnung. In 80 Phrasen um die Welt", 01. Juli 2020.

Lee, Kuam Yew; From Third World to First, 2016.

Lévi-Strauss, Claude; Das wilde Denken, 1976.

Li Xuanmin and Fan Anqi; Government of China „White paper", in Global Times China, 19. Januar 2023, https://www.globaltimes.cn//author/Reporter -Li-Xuanmin.html.

Lieven, Dominic (ed.); The Cambridge History of Russia, 2005.

Lohmann, Sascha; in SWP-Aktuell 2019/A 31, Mai 2019, Extraterritoriale US-Sanktionen.

Lorenz, Konrad und Wuketits, Franz (Hg.): Die Evolution des Denkens. Zwölf Beiträge, 1983.

Lorenz, Konrad; Das sogenannte Böse: Zur Naturgeschichte der Aggression, 1963.

Lovelock, James; Gaia. A New Look at Life on Earth, 1972.

Lukács, Georg; Die Zerstörung der Vernunft, 1955.

Mackinder, Halford; Artikel „The Geographical Pivot of History, 1904.

Mahlmann, Matthias; Philosophische Grundlehren, 7. Auflage, 2022. https://www.rwi.uzh.ch/elt-lst-mahlmann/rechtstheorie/kant/de/html/unit_u 2.html.

Marschall, Tim; The Future of Gegography, 2023.

Mausfeld, Rainer; Warum schweigen die Lämmer?, 2018.

Mayer, Thomas; Die Ordnung der Freiheit und ihre Feinde: Vom Aufstand der Verlassenen gegen die Herrschaft der Eliten, 2018.

Meadows, H. Donella; Thinking in Systems, 2008.

Mereschkowski, Dmitri; Leonardo da Vinci, 1951.

Merk, Frederick; Manifest Destiny and Mission in American History: A Reinterpretation, 1963.

Mises, Ludwig von; Human Action: A Treatise on Economics, 1949.

Mises, Ludwig von; Theorie des Geldes und der Umlaufmittel, 1912.

Mises, Ludwig von; Vom Wert der besseren Ideen, Vorlesungen, 1958.

Mittasch, Alwin; Von der Chemie zur Philosophie, 1948.

Mohr, Daniel; „Viele amerikanische Investoren, Der Dax ist fest in ausländischer Hand", FAZ vom 26.01.2017.

Morland, Paul; The Power of Demography to Understand Our World, 2019.

Mumford, Lewis; The Original American edition: The Transformation of Man, 1956.

Mumford, Lewis; Mythos der Maschine. Kultur, Technik und Macht, 1986.

Mumford, Lewis; Technics and Civilization, 1934.

Mumford, Lewis; The Condition of Man, 1944.

Mumford, Lewis; The Culture of Cities, 1938.

Mumford, Lewis; The Story of Utopias, 1922.

Needham, Joseph; Moulds of Understanding, 1976.

Needham, Joseph; Needham Research Institute, Science and Civilisation in China, since 1954.

Needham, Joseph; Wissenschaftlicher Universalismus, 1979, das Kapitel „Der Zeitbegriff im Orient", s. 176-250.

Neubauer, Heinz; Grundlagen der Systemtheorie, 1989.

Nietzsche, Friedrich; Genealogie der Moral, 1887.

Pany, Thomas; Syrien-Krise und EU: Katastrophale Armut und Auswanderung als letzter Ausweg, 22. Februar 2024.

Perry, Markus; Understanding Organizational Culture: A Systems Theory Perspective, 2023.

Pfluger, Walter; Ronga – Ein Beispiel politischer Komplementarität, 1987.

Popper, Karl; The Open Society and its Enemies, 1945. Deutsche Ausgabe in 2 Bänden, „Die offene Gesellschaft und ihre Feinde", 1957 und 1958.

Prigogine, Ilya; Order through Fluctuation. Self-Organization and Social System, 1976.

Reid, Anna; Borderland, A Journey Through the History of the Ukraine, 2015.

Reinhard, Wolfgang; Die Unterwerfung der Welt: Globalgeschichte der europäischen Expansion 1414 – 2015, 2017.

Richard, Wilhelm; Weisheit des Ostens, von 1951.

Riemann, Fritz; Basic Forms of Fear. A depth psychological study, 1975.

Richter, Horst-Eberhard; Flüchten oder Standhalten, 2012.

Richter, Horst-Eberhard; Moral in Zeiten der Krise, Originalausgabe 2010.

Riegel, Tobias; Syrien – Die unendliche (Lügen-)Geschichte", 20. Februar 2020.

Riemann, Fritz; Grundformen der Angst. Eine tiefenpsychologische Studie. 10. überarbeitete und erweiterte Auflage, 1975.

Risk Management Network, Neue Ära der Großmachtkonflikte – Erosionsprozesse der geopolitischen Welt, am 7. Oktober 2019. https://www.risknet.de/themen/risknews/ero sionsprozesse-der-geopolitischen-welt/.

Rübel, Gerhard; Grundlagen der monetären Aussenwirtschaft, 2009.

Rügemer, Werner; Die Kapitalisten des 21. Jahrhunderts. Allgemeinverständliche Notizen zum Aufstieg der neuen Finanzakteure, 2018.

Rügemer, Werner; USA im Niedergang? – Aber in der EU so mächtig wie noch nie, Artikel im Online Magazin „Nachdenkseiten" vom 23. April 2019.

Sachs, Jeffry; Agenda der US-Aussenpolitik", am 20. Dezember 2023, auf dem Online Magazin Telepolis: https://www.telepolis.de/features/Kriegsdeba kel-und-viel-Geld-Die-geheime-Agenda-hinter-der-gescheiterten-US-Aussenpolitik-9584068.html?seite=all.

Sachs, Jeffry; https://www.jeffsachs.org/newspaper-articles/

Sakwa, Richard; Frontline Ukraine: Crisis in the Borderlands, 2022.

Sakwa, Richard; The Lost Peace: How the West Failed to prevent a Second Cold War, 2023.

Sakwa, Richard; Wir sind an der Beerdigung der alten Schule der Diplomatie, Interview vom 21. Mai 2024 in GlobalBridge.

Schmalz, Stefan und Ebenau, Mathias; Auf dem Sprung – Brasilien, Indien und China, 2011.

Schmalz, Stefan; Chinas neue Rolle im globalen Kapitalismus. in: Prokla 40 (4):483-503, 2015.

Schöllgen, Gregor; Das Zeitalter des Imperialismus (in Oldenbourg, Grundriss der Geschichte, Band 15), 2000.

Schuldt, Christian; Zeitalter der Krisen, Bundesverband „Energie, Wasser, Leben", 2021.

Sieren, Frank und Vossenkuhl, Josef, et al; "Zukunft? China! Wie die neue Supermacht unser Leben, unsere Politik, unsere Wirtschaft verändert", 2020.

Sieren, Frank; Shenzhen – Zukunft Made in China: Zwischen Kreativität und Kontrolle, 2021.

Sigrist, Christian; Regulierte Anarchie, 1967.

Sinn, Hans-Werner; Der Mythos vom Marshall-Plan, 03.02.2023. https://www.hanswernersinn.de/de/marshallplan-brackmann-hb-03022023

Sinn, Hans-Werner; https://www.hanswernersinn.de/de.

SIPRI – Stockholm International Peace Research Institute. SIPRI: https://www.sipri.org/databases/armstransfers.

Smith, Adam; Der Wohlstand der Nationen, Erstveröffentlichung 1776.

Spangler, David; The Flame of Incarnation, First edition, 2009.

Spengler, Oswald; Der Untergang des Abendlandes, erster Band 1918, zweiter Band 1922.
Spethmann, Dieter; Deutschland verschenkt seinen Wohlstand, am 19.01.2011 in der FAZ.

Spykman, Nicholas J.; Geography and Foreign Policy", published in The American Political Science Review, Vol. XXXII, Nos. 1 and 2, February and April 1938.

Steinbuch, Karl; Falsch programmiert – Über das Versagen unserer Gesellschaft in der Gegenwart und vor der Zukunft, 1968.

Steiner, Rudolf; Band GA 335 der Gesamtausgabe.

Steiner, Rudolf; Gesamtausgabe Band GA 185, Vorträge von 1918.

Stephanson, Anders; Manifest Destiny: American Expansionism and the Empire of Right, 1995.

Straubhaar, Thomas; Der Untergang ist abgesagt: Wider die Mythen des Demographischen Wandels, 2016.

Thomas, Anthony; Rhodes: the Race for Africa, 1997.

Tiger, Lionel und Fox, Robin; The Imperial Animal, 1976.

Todd, Emmanuel; La Défaite de l'Occident, von 2024.

Todd, Emmanuel; Weltmacht USA: ein Nachruf, 2003.

Tofler, Alvin ; Revolutionary Wealth, 2006.

Toynbee, Arnold J.; Essay aus dem Jahre 1934. "Things Not Foreseen at Paris; The Future in Retrospect".

Vidal, Gore; Perpetual War for Perpetual Peace: How we got to be so hated. American Imperialism, Book 1", 2002.

Wallerstein, Immanuel; Aufstieg und zukünftiger Niedergang des kapitalistischen Weltsystems. Zur Grundlegung vergleichender Analyse. In: Senghaas, Dieter (Hrsg.): Kapitalistische Weltökonomie. Kontroversen über ihren Ursprung und ihre Entwicklungsdynamik, 1979 und 1982.

Wallerstein, Immanuel; The Capitalist World-Economy, 1979.

Wang, Mingyuan; Why Have Repeated Efforts to Revitalize the Northeast Failed? – Rethinking the Twentieth Anniversary of the Strategy of Revitalizing the Old Industrial base. https://www.readingthechinadream.com/wang-mingyuan-on-chinas-northeast.html.

Warburg, Paul M.; The Federal Reserve System: its origin and growth; reflections and recollections; 2 volumes, New York 1930.

Weidenhausen, Gerd; Buchbesprechung, in Die Drei, Nr. 5.: Wolfgang Bittner, Die Eroberung Europas durch die USA, 2015.

Wendt, Reinhard; Vom Kolonialismus zur Globalisierung: Europa und die Welt seit 1500, 2016.

Wiener, Norbert; The Human Use of Human Beings – Cybernetics and Society, 1950.

Wilhelm, Richard; Die Seele Chinas, 1925.

Willke, Hellmut; Global Governance, 2006.

Willke, Helmut; Atopia, 2001.

Wulf, Andrea; Alexander von Humboldt und die Erfindung der Natur, deutsch 2016.

Wüthrich, Werner; Europäische Integration, in dem Schweizer Magazin «Zeit-Fragen» von 2011 bis 2012.

Zeit-Fragen, Nr. 38, 2010: Studie zur „Geschichte der EU – Teil 1.

Zhao, Tingyang; Alles unter einem Himmel - Vergangenheit und Zukunft der Weltordnung, 2019.

ZHAO, Tingyang; All under Heaven: The Tianxia System for a Possible World Order, 2016.

Zürcher Kantonalbank, CBO, Census, OMB. https://www.zkb.ch/de/blog/anlegen/us-staatsverschuldung-rekordkurs.html.

Zürn, Michael; A Theory of Global Governance: Authority, Legitimacy and Contestation, 2018.